Letts
gets you through

KS2 GRAMMAR & PUNCTUATION SATs SUCCESS TOPIC WORKBOOK

Ages 9–11

KS2

GRAMMAR & PUNCTUATION

SATs

TOPIC WORKBOOK

LAURA GRIFFITHS

About this book

Grammar and punctuation

Grammar and punctuation are a key focus of the new primary curriculum. They are crucial English skills that will enable your child to communicate effectively in school and in later life. Developing these skills will help your child to convey clear and accurate information when speaking and writing.

This book separates grammar from punctuation and breaks them down topic by topic, offering clear explanations and practice at each step. It will also aid preparation for the Key Stage 2 **English Grammar, Punctuation and Spelling** test.

Features of the book

- The *Key to grammar* and *Key to punctuation* sections introduce each topic through concise explanations and clear examples.

- *Practice activities* include a variety of tasks to see how well your child has grasped each concept.

- *Test your grammar* and *Test your punctuation* provide focused questions after both sections.

- A *mixed test* at the end of the book helps to cement your child's overall understanding of the grammar and punctuation topics covered.

- *Answers* are in a pull-out booklet at the centre of the book.

Grammar and punctuation tips

- Spend time reading and looking through books (both fiction and non-fiction), asking your child to identify examples of different types of grammar and punctuation. For example, play 'finding an adjective' or 'spotting speech marks', or talk about why a new paragraph has started.

- Encourage your child to write by making diaries, recipe cards, stories and letters together. Encourage them to use the correct punctuation in their own writing.

- Make grammar and punctuation fun. For example, play games like *I spy* but start with: 'I am thinking of a noun beginning with…' or a charades-type game where your child can act out an adverb.

Contents

Sentence types

Sentences can be categorised as **statements**, **questions**, **exclamations** or **commands**:

Sentence type	Definition	End punctuation
Statement	A sentence that gives information.	full stop (.)
Question	A sentence that needs an answer.	question mark (?)
Exclamation	A sentence that shows emotion.	exclamation mark (!)
Command	A sentence (without a subject) that tells someone to do something.	full stop (.) or exclamation mark (!)

Sentences can also be categorised as **simple**, **compound** or **complex**:

Sentence type	Definition	Example
Simple sentence	A sentence with one clause.	The boy ate his tea.
Compound sentence	A sentence with two or more main clauses, usually joined together with a coordinating conjunction (e.g. for, and, nor, but, or, yet).	The boy ate his tea and he had a drink.
Complex sentence	A sentence with a main clause and one or more subordinate clauses. (Subordinate clauses do not make sense on their own.)	The boy, who was feeling very hungry, ate his tea.

1. Read the sentences below and write whether they are a **statement**, **question**, **exclamation** or **command**.

    a) Which way do we go now? _question_

    b) Take the next road on the left. _command_

    c) The village is 20 miles away. _statement_

    exclamation

    d) I can't wait to see it! _____

2. Read the sentences below and write whether they are **simple**, **compound** or **complex** sentences.

a) I went swimming last night. _simple_

b) Although I like watching football, I prefer to play rugby.
complex

c) I had finished all my homework, so I was allowed to play outside.
complex

d) The flowers, which looked like they were dying, needed some water.
complex

e) I can name all the planets. _simple_

f) I bought a new pair of shorts and my sister bought some shoes.
compound

g) While I was playing the piano, my dad was strumming his guitar.
complex

3. Write three sentences of your own: a **simple**, **compound** and **complex** one.

a) (simple) _I went to a party. My brother painted the door. Two leaves were flying in the air_

b) (compound) _The girl bought the guitar and played it. The boy went to the gym and got stronger. The dog had a bath and it was smelling better._

c) (complex) _The girl who was starving ate an apple. The boy who climbed on the roof so he fell of it. Jake, who was very hot, got out in so much trouble._

Subject and verb agreement

Key to grammar

Most sentences have a **subject** and a **verb.** The subject is normally the person or thing that is doing the action. The verb is the doing (or sometimes being) word.

You play cricket with a bat and ball.

subject verb

You need to be sure that the subject correctly **agrees** with the verb.

✓	✗
I like cricket.	**I likes** cricket.
You are learning to play.	**You is** learning to play.
The **girl looks** for the ball.	The **girl look** for the ball.
We **play** cricket.	We **plays** cricket.

Practice activities

1. Which sentences are grammatically correct?

Tick **two**

We is going to the shops. ☒

The children have gone to the lake. ✓

I done my homework. ☒

You drive really well. ✓

They spends the most money. ☒

The man know a lot about computers. ☒

Subject and verb agreement

2. Put a circle around the correct form of the verb in each sentence.

a) Sarah and Tamara **have** / **has** brown hair.

b) My brother **ride** / **rides** his bike all the time.

c) You **play** / **plays** on your computer every night.

d) I **is** / **am** going to put the rubbish in the bin.

3. Rewrite these sentences, changing either the form of the subject or the form of the verb, so that they agree.

Example: The monkey swing through the trees.

Two possible answers: The monkey swing**s** through the trees *or* The monkey**s** swing through the trees.

a) The sheep dog are chasing the flock of sheep.

The sheep dog is chasing the flock of sheep.

b) The shops is closing for lunch and will reopen at 2pm.

The shop is closing for lunch and will reopen at 2pm.

c) The babies keeps crying because they wants some more milk.

The babies keep crying because they want some more milk.

d) The children has finished the game.

The child had finished the game.

e) The bag of sandwiches were left behind this morning.

The bag of sandwich was left behind this morning.

Nouns

Key to grammar

A **noun** is a word that names a person, place, animal or thing. There are four different types of noun.

Proper nouns name a particular place, person, time or event and begin with a capital letter. For example:

> **Christmas**   **Thomas**   **January**   **Greece**

Common nouns are general words for **kinds** of people, animals, places or things. For example:

> **girl**   **horse**   **shop**   **apple**

Collective nouns name **groups** of people, animals, places or things. For example:

> a **pride** of lions   a **pack** of cards

Abstract nouns refer to things that **cannot be sensed**. For example:

> **sleep**   **peace**   **love**

Practice activities

1. Write **PN** (proper noun), **CN** (common noun) or **COLN** (collective noun) above each noun written in bold in the sentences below.

    a) **Jenna** loved the **film** she watched at the **cinema**.

    b) **Paris** is the capital **city** of **France**.

    c) The football **team** was nervous before the **match**.

    d) **Mr James** went to the **dentist** for a new **filling**.

2. Use the collective nouns below to complete these sentences. You can only use each word once.

crowd	bunch	gang	pack	swarm	herd

a) A _____ of bees buzzed around my head.

b) Last night a _____ of thieves broke into the jewellery shop.

c) A _____ of elephants had arrived at the zoo.

d) We are going to play with this _____ of cards.

e) A _____ of people gathered to watch the show.

f) I put a _____ of grapes in my shopping basket.

3. Put the nouns below into the correct column in the table.

dog	chair	insect	train	Mrs Green
flock		misery	kindness	Julia
gaggle		Thursday	New Zealand	boy

Proper nouns	Common nouns	Collective nouns	Abstract nouns

Adjectives

An adjective is a word that **describes** a noun or a pronoun (for example, good, bad, light and dark).

Comparative adjectives compare **two nouns**. If the adjective has one syllable, then in most cases you need to add **er**. Here is an example using **slow** (a one-syllable adjective):

> The bus is **slower** than the train.

However, if the adjective has two syllables or more, the word **more** or the word **less** should be placed in front of it. Here is an example using **colourful** (a three-syllable adjective):

> The parrot was **more colourful** than the other birds.

Superlative adjectives compare **more than two nouns**. If the adjective has one syllable, you usually add **est**. If it has two syllables or more, the word **most** or the word **least** should usually be placed in front of it. For example:

> The bus is the **slowest**.
>
> The blackbird is the **least colourful**.

Watch out for exceptions. For example:

Adjective	Comparative	Superlative
good (one syllable)	better	best
hungry (two syllables)	hungrier	hungriest

Practice activities

1. Underline the adjectives in each sentence.

   a) Dad was very proud of his fast, new, shiny car.

   b) The rough sea crashed against the jagged, grey rocks.

2. Change these adjectives into **comparatives** and then place them in one of the sentences below. Decide whether to add the word 'more' or simply change the ending of each adjective. Use each word only once.

intelligent	new	green	beautiful

a) Her scooter is _____ than mine.

b) My sister is _____ than she thinks.

c) I am _____ than my brother.

d) This plant is _____ than that one.

3. Change each adjective in brackets into a **superlative** and write a sentence for each. Watch out, some may be exceptions to the rule!

a) (brave) _____

_____

b) (bad) _____

_____

c) (honest) _____

_____

d) (friendly) _____

_____

Pronouns

Key to grammar

Personal pronouns, which take the place of a noun, can vary depending on whether they are the subject or object of a sentence.

Subject	I	you	she	he	it	we	they
Object	me	you	her	him	it	us	them

Possessive pronouns tell us who or what owns something that has already been mentioned. For example:

These six oranges are **mine**.

Those seven apples are **yours**.

That juicy melon is **ours**.

Relative pronouns link a subordinate clause to the rest of a sentence.

that	which	who	whom	whose
whichever		whoever		whomever

For example, I like the book **that** you have chosen.

Demonstrative pronouns are used to refer to objects or people that have already been mentioned. For example:

"I don't usually like flowers, but I love **these**!"

"What a mess! Who did **this**?"

Practice activities

1. Look at the words in bold in the sentences below and write **personal**, **possessive**, **relative** or **demonstrative** in the spaces provided.

   a) Alex played with a yellow football. It was **his**. _____

   b) Sarah and **I** had lunch together. _____

   c) I grew up in the 1980s. **Those** were the days! _____

   d) The banana, **which** was ripe, was ready to eat. _____

2. Rewrite these sentences, replacing the words in bold with a correct pronoun.

a) Preta ate a sandwich. **The sandwich** was delicious.

_____

_____

b) Eliza danced for ages at the disco. **Eliza** ached from head to toe when **the disco** had finished.

_____

_____

c) Mum asked us to put our shoes on, but **the shoes** were dirty.

_____

d) At my aunt's house there is a cat called Maple. **The cat** is **my aunt's**.

_____

_____

3. Add suitable pronouns to each sentence.

a) The pirates, _____ lived on a faraway island, were looking for treasure.

b) The photographer needs all these people to sit down and smile at _____.

c) I will come to your house, so we can do our homework together. We will finish _____ quickly.

d) Matthew and _____ argued because _____ said I had cheated in the game.

Prepositions

Key to grammar

Prepositions are words that show the relationship between nouns or pronouns. They can show position according to **place** or **time**.

PLACE

The girl put the hat **on** the snowman.

The cat sat **under** the tree.

TIME

My mum clapped **after** the performance.

We left **before** midnight.

Practice activities

1. Underline the prepositions in the sentences below and write whether they show **time** or **place**.

    a) He couldn't see the tomato sauce on the table. _____

    b) The baby ate before sleeping. _____

    c) I looked around the room for a friendly smile. _____

    d) I go swimming after gymnastics. _____

    e) The troll stomped across the bridge. _____

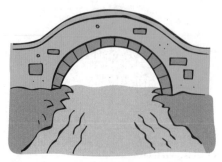

Prepositions

2. Complete each sentence with a suitable preposition.

a) Our head teacher read a story _____ assembly today.

b) The cat leapt _____ the wall, then he jumped _____ it.

c) Emily jumped _____ the trampoline.

d) Our family like to eat dessert _____ the main course.

e) Dad was downstairs working _____ his garage.

f) When the bread was ready, the baker put it _____ the table to cool.

3. Rewrite these sentences correctly by changing the preposition.

a) To score a goal, the ball must go up the line.

_____

b) The children ate their dinner up the table.

_____

c) We cycled through the lake.

_____

d) I put my shopping at the basket.

_____

Modal verbs

Key to grammar

The main modal verbs are **will**, **would**, **can**, **could**, **may**, **might**, **shall**, **should**, **must** and **ought**.

Modal verbs can express necessity, uncertainty, ability or permission.

less certain

↓

more certain

I **might** do my homework.

I **should** do my homework.

I **will** do my homework.

To talk about the past using a modal verb we add **have + the past participle of the verb** (often the form of the verb ending in **ed**).

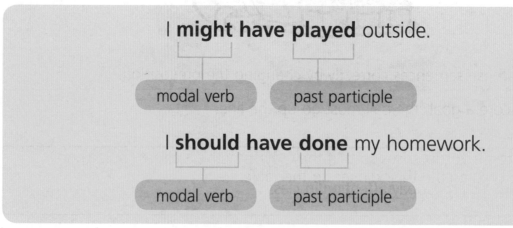

I **might have played** outside.

modal verb   past participle

I **should have done** my homework.

modal verb   past participle

Practice activities

1. Put a circle around the modal verb in each sentence.

    a) Shall we go out for dinner tonight?

    b) We could have caught the bus.

    c) They should work harder in training.

    d) The kittens would have been hungry if you hadn't fed them.

    e) You might see me because I will be wearing a red top hat.

2. Circle the correct modal verbs below so that the sentences make sense.

   a) He really **should / ought** save some money.

   b) If you want to go ice skating, you **ought / will** need to hire some skates.

   c) I **ought / shall** to go to bed earlier because I am always tired.

3. Complete these sentences so that they say something about your school.

   Example: You must <u>pay attention in class</u>.

   a) You ought to _____ .

   b) You can _____ .

   c) You should _____ .

4. Complete these sentences using a **different noun** and a **different modal verb** at the beginning of each.

   Example: <u>Tomorrow will</u> be cold.

   a) _____ be good.

   b) _____ be exciting.

   c) _____ be boring.

   d) _____ be dangerous.

Phrases

Key to grammar

Phrases are small groups of words (or just one word) that form part of a sentence. The three important types are noun phrases, verb phrases and prepositional phrases.

Noun phrases have a noun (or a pronoun) as the main word. For example:

shoes	the shoes	the old pair of shoes
me	silly old me	

Verb phrases have a verb as the main word. For example:

eat	is eating	does not eat	has eaten
	has been eaten	can eat	should eat
	want to eat	go to eat	

Prepositional phrases begin with a preposition and are followed by a noun phrase. For example:

on the table	against the grey rocks
round the sharp bend	opposite him
by your dog	after the game

Practice activities

1. Look at the phrases below and write whether they are a **noun phrase**, **verb phrase** or **prepositional phrase**.

    a) along the water's edge _____

    b) went to sleep _____

    c) the shop _____

2. Underline the **noun phrase(s)** in each sentence.

   a) The cat jumped.

   b) Catch the red bus.

   c) Poor Dorothy coughed.

   d) The car broke down but the old van continued.

3. Underline the **verb phrase** in each sentence.

   a) The classroom has been tidied.

   b) The experienced walkers can climb up a mountain.

   c) My dad is cutting the grass.

   d) This piece of jigsaw does not fit anywhere.

4. Use the prepositions below to help you complete the sentences with a **prepositional phrase**. You can use each preposition more than once.

before	on	at	during

   a) The car broke down _____.

   b) The children were playing _____.

   c) The lights went out _____.

   d) _____, I must put my bike in the garage.

Expanded noun phrases

Key to grammar

Detail can be added to a sentence by **expanding** a noun phrase.

One way of doing this is by **adding adjectives**. For example:

> Paul kicked the ball. ⟶ Paul kicked the **bouncy**, **blue** ball.

Another way is by **adding a prepositional phrase**. For example:

> Paul kicked the bouncy, blue ball. ⟶ Paul kicked the bouncy, blue ball **in the park**.

You can also add an **adverbial phrase**. For example:

> Paul kicked the bouncy, blue ball in the park. ⟶ Paul kicked the bouncy, blue ball in the park **this morning**.

In this way a sentence can be built up in stages. For example:

> The dog.
> The clever dog.
> The clever dog found a stick.
> The clever dog found an old stick.
> The clever dog found an old stick in the park.
> The clever dog found an old stick in the park this morning.

Expanded noun phrases

Practice activities

1. Expand the noun phrases in the sentences below. Use an adjective, a prepositional phrase and an adverbial phrase at least once.

    a) Alex watched TV.

    _____

    b) The boys played.

    _____

    c) Kiera wore a dress.

    _____

    d) The cat jumped.

    _____

    e) The bed is comfy.

    _____

2. Add an expanded noun phrase to complete these sentences.

    a) Michael ran up the hill towards _____

    b) We enjoy playing outside in the _____

    c) I am having a sleepover at _____

    d) Martha caught the train for _____

    e) The news reporter recorded the _____

Adverbs

Key to grammar

Adverbs are used to tell us more about a **verb**.

They often tell us **how**, **when** or **where** something happens or is done.

The girl skipped **quickly**.

The bus **finally** arrived.

Many adverbs can be formed by adding the suffix **ly** to an adjective. For example:

quick	$\longrightarrow$	quickly
slow	$\longrightarrow$	slowly
easy	$\longrightarrow$	easily

Practice activities

1. Underline the adverb(s) in each sentence.

    a) The car stopped abruptly at the traffic lights.

    b) Angrily, Dad slammed the door.

    c) Zara waited patiently to see the doctor.

    d) The snow fell heavily as the children excitedly threw snowballs at each other.

2. Write the adverb that can be made from each adjective.

Example: quick ⟶ _____quickly_____

a) loud ⟶ _____

b) beautiful ⟶ _____

c) gentle ⟶ _____

d) even ⟶ _____

e) smooth ⟶ _____

f) lazy ⟶ _____

3. Add **one** adverb to each sentence. Use each adverb once only.

gracefully	**carefully**	**slowly**	**sneakily**
urgently	**nervously**	**eagerly**	

a) The head teacher wanted to talk to my parents _____.

b) _____, we waited for our test results.

c) _____, the car rolled down the hill.

d) _____, I wrapped the delicate vase in bubble wrap, so it wouldn't break.

e) The ducks ate the bread _____ because they were hungry.

f) Our cat _____ ate some of the chicken when no one was looking.

g) The ballerina _____ jumped into the air.

Adverbial phrases

Key to grammar

Whereas an **adverb** is a single word, an **adverbial phrase** is a **group of words** that can be used to tell us more about a verb. It often tells us **where, when, how, why, with whom, how long** or **how often** something is done. For example:

when:
> He played tennis **yesterday afternoon**.

how:
> The girl ate her breakfast **really quickly**.

Adverbial phrases can also be prepositional phrases. For example:

where:
> The boy threw a ball **over the fence**.

with whom:
> The boy threw a ball **with his sister**.

Adverbial phrases can be written before or after a verb. If they are used at the start of a sentence they are followed by a comma and are called **fronted adverbials**. For example:

> **Yesterday afternoon,** he played tennis.

Practice activities

1. Underline the adverbial phrase in each sentence and write whether it shows **where**, **how often** or **how** something is done.

    a) The weather forecast says it will rain every day this week.

    _____

    b) The Smith family walk to school extremely slowly. _____

    c) Very loudly, the orchestra started to play. _____

    d) Lois and Kai played on the swings at the park. _____

2. Write **fronted adverbial phrases** at the start of the sentences below. Remember that an adverbial phrase must contain **more** than one word.

Example: <u>With his sharp little teeth</u>, the mouse nibbled the cheese.

a) _____, the cat prowled around the garden.

b) _____, the gun went off.

c) _____, he crossed the finishing line.

3. Write some sentences containing adverbial phrases. Remember to vary the position of the adverbial phrases. When you have finished, **underline each adverbial phrase**.

a) _____

_____

b) _____

_____

c) _____

_____

Adverbials of time and possibility

Key to grammar

An **adverbial of time** is a type of adverb or adverbial phrase. It is used to give more information about the **time** or **frequency** of an action.

Adverbials of time are useful to use in your writing because they give added detail, provide chronological sequencing and can move stories forwards or create flashbacks. For example:

> **Eventually**, he arrived at the house. He **rarely** visited it as it made him sad, but **lately** he had started to feel that **sooner or later** he must do so.

Adverbials of possibility show how certain we are about something. Common ones are: **certainly**, **definitely**, **maybe**, **perhaps** and **possibly**.

> It will **certainly** take a long time, will **probably** be difficult, but **maybe** I will try it.

Practice activities

1. Circle all the **adverbials of time**.

    after a while   beautifully   previously

        soon   tightly   quietly   before

    instantly   openly   immediately   secretly

2. Complete these sentences with an adverbial of time.

    a) We expect our cousins to arrive _____.

    b) _____, the sun was shining.

    c) My mum can pick us up _____.

Adverbials of time and possibility

3. Sort the adverbials below into adverbials of time and adverbials of possibility.

certainly   soon   afterwards   possibly   seldom

next week   maybe   perhaps   last night   all day

Adverbials of time	Adverbials of possibility

4. Add a different adverbial of possibility to each sentence to make them correct.

a) It is _____ going to rain.

b) My friends will _____ come to play at my house.

c) _____ I will be chosen to sing a solo.

d) I will _____ be watching the football match on Saturday.

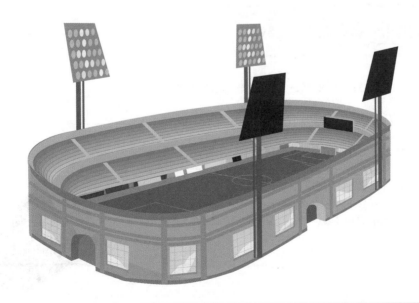

Clauses 1

Key to grammar

A **clause** is a group of words that contains at least one **subject** and one **verb**. For example:

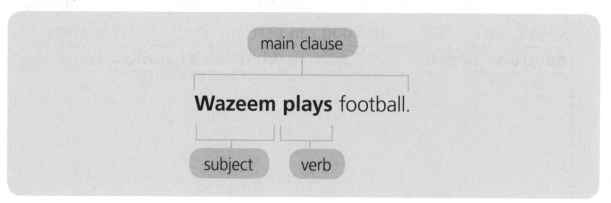

A **main clause** is a complete sentence that makes sense by itself.

Subordinate clauses still have a subject and a verb, but they start with a **subordinating conjunction** and so do not make sense on their own. They need to be paired with a main clause. For example:

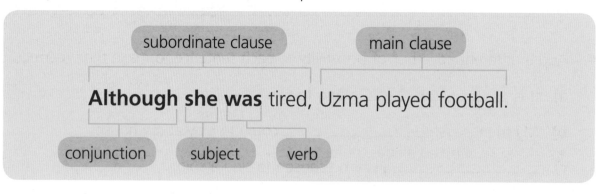

Practice activities

1. Underline the **main clause** in each sentence.

   a) The baby drank some milk.

   b) The boy sat down until the bus arrived.

   c) Because he was tired, Jonah went to bed.

   d) I must wear my hat as it is a hot day.

2. Decide if each clause is a main or subordinate clause and write it in the correct place in the table.

before we left   **I baked a cake**   **because we are on holiday**

we will have a BBQ   **our dog can perform tricks**   **if it is sunny**

Main clauses	Subordinate clauses

3. Complete these sentences by adding a **main clause**.

a) After he worked all day, _____

b) Although it was his birthday, _____

c) _____ because he was slow.

d) _____ while she ate her tea.

4. Complete the sentence below by adding a **subordinate clause**.

The girl cried _____

_____

Clauses 2

Key to grammar

If the main clause comes before the subordinate clause, a comma is **not** needed. If a subordinate clause comes first, a comma **is** needed. For example:

> I was worried because I had forgotten my homework.
>
> Because I had forgotten my homework, I was worried.

Relative clauses are subordinate clauses that start with a relative pronoun (e.g. **who, whom, which, that, whose**) or a relative adverb (e.g. **where, when, why**). In a relative clause, the relative pronoun or adverb acts as the subject of the verb.

A relative clause can sometimes come in the middle of a main clause. For example:

> The teacher, **who works with Year 6**, is very interesting.

Practice activities

1. Which sentences below use a **comma** correctly?

   Tick **two**

   I got up early, because I had a lot to prepare. ☐

   Because the last bus had gone, I walked home. ☐

   I was tired so, I didn't stay late. ☐

   Although I like most fruit, I don't like bananas. ☐

2. Underline the **relative clause** in each sentence.

    a) Yesterday, I went out with my friend, who is already twelve.

    b) The cakes, which were left on the table, were delicious.

    c) The Internet, which is a great invention, helps me with my homework.

    d) The acrobat, who performs impressive moves, will be on stage shortly.

    e) In the south of England, where the climate is usually warmer, the spring flowers are already in bloom.

3. Choose a word from the box below to fill the spaces in the sentences.

whose	where	which	who

    a) The house, _____ was empty, was for sale.

    b) My grandmother, _____ is nearly ninety, struggles to walk.

    c) The cricket ground, _____ international matches are held, is near my house.

    d) The dog, _____ lead had been lost, wanted to go for a walk.

4. Write a relative clause for the sentence below.

The man, _____,
ran into the burning building.

Complex sentences

Key to grammar

A **complex sentence** is a sentence that contains a **main (independent) clause** and at least one **subordinate (dependent) clause**. No matter which clause is used first, it is still called a complex sentence.

complex sentence

The children sat down because they were told to.

main clause · subordinate clause

This sentence also works with the main clause **after** the subordinate.

complex sentence

Because they were told to, the children sat down.

subordinate clause · main clause

A subordinate clause can also be put in the middle of a main clause.

subordinate (relative) clause

Michelle, who was very tall and athletic, enjoyed PE lessons.

main clause

A complex sentence can also have more than one subordinate clause.

subordinate clause 1 · subordinate clause 2

Because he likes them, Isaac writes poems that rhyme.

main clause

Practice activities

1. Underline the **two subordinate clauses** in each sentence.

   a) The boy, who was cycling, was on his way to school, which was two miles away.

   b) The classroom, which is usually tidy, was a mess because the children had been painting.

   c) Because they were going to a party, the twins were allowed to stay up late, which was a very rare occurrence.

2. Write three complex sentences using **one** subordinate clause in each. Try to vary where you put the subordinate clause in each sentence.

   a) _____

   _____

   b) _____

   _____

   c) _____

   _____

3. Write a complex sentence using **two** subordinate clauses.

   _____

   _____

   _____

Determiners

Key to grammar

A **determiner** stands before a noun or noun phrase. The most common determiners are **the**, **a** and **an**. They are also known as **articles**.

The **definite article** is **the**. It is normally used when we are talking about a particular thing. For example:

> **the** piano　　　　**the** egg　　　　**the** new school

The **indefinite** article is **a** or **an**. These are normally used when we are talking about a thing in general. For example:

> **a** piano　　　　**an** egg　　　　**a** new school

We use **a** before a word beginning with a consonant and **an** before a word beginning with a vowel. Words beginning with a silent **h** are exceptions. We use **an** before them because they have a vowel sound. For example:

> **a** hospital *(h is not silent)*　　　　**an** hour *(h is silent)*

Practice activities

1. Underline the **determiners** in the sentences below.

   a) The people, who were waiting at the bus stop, wanted the next bus to be red.

   b) An artist, who painted in the style of Van Gogh, once entered his work in an exhibition.

   c) A local choir beat a flautist, a clarinettist and a pianist to win first prize at the National Music Festival.

2. Which sentence uses the correct **determiner**?

Tick **one**

We eat the cake every day. ☐

A octopus has eight legs. ☐

She travels into the London every day for work. ☐

He wanted to buy a new car. ☐

3. Choose **a**, **an** or **the** to fill in the gaps in the sentences below.

a) Although _____ tide was coming in, we still managed to have some time playing on _____ beach.

b) On Saturday _____ weather will be humid with _____ thunderstorm likely.

c) Mum asked us to shut _____ windows because _____ rain was coming in.

d) _____ African elephant has larger ears than _____ Asian elephant.

e) Our class went on _____ visit to _____ science museum in London.

f) My sister screamed when she saw _____ large, hairy spider crawl across her bedroom.

Double negatives

Key to grammar

Double negatives are often used in **dialogue**. They should **not** be used in **Standard English** as they are grammatically incorrect and can be quite confusing.

A double negative is when two negative words in a sentence cancel each other out. For example:

> He **can't** play with **nobody**.

The sentence above is incorrect. When written correctly in Standard English, the sentence should be:

> He **can't** play with **anyone / anybody**.

or

> He **can** play with **no one**.

Practice activities

1. Tick the sentences that are grammatically correct and put a cross next to the ones that are grammatically incorrect.

	Tick/Cross
I don't listen to anyone.	
You're not going nowhere.	
The baby can't hardly talk yet.	
Don't get into any trouble.	
You're not going anywhere.	
The baby can hardly talk yet.	
Don't get into no trouble.	
I don't listen to no one.	

Answers

Pages 4–5
1. **a)** question **b)** command **c)** statement
   d) exclamation
2. **a)** simple **b)** complex **c)** compound
   d) complex **e)** simple **f)** compound
   g) complex
3. **Accept any correct sentences, for example:**
   a) I like chocolate.
   b) I like chocolate and I like fruit.
   c) Although I like chocolate, I prefer eating sweets.

Pages 6–7
1. The children have gone to the lake; You drive really well.
2. **a)** have **b)** rides **c)** play **d)** am
3. **a)** The **sheep dog is / sheep dogs are** chasing the flock of sheep.
   b) The **shops are / shop is** closing for lunch and will reopen at 2pm.
   c) The **babies keep crying / baby keeps crying** because **they want / it wants** some more milk.
   d) The **children have / child has** finished the game.
   e) The **bag of sandwiches was / bags of sandwiches were** left behind this morning.

Pages 8–9
1. **a)** Jenna (**PN**) film (**CN**) cinema (**CN**)
   b) Paris (**PN**) city (**CN**) France (**PN**)
   c) team (**COLN**) match (**CN**)
   d) Mr James (**PN**) dentist (**CN**) filling (**CN**)
2. **a)** swarm **b)** gang **c)** herd
   d) pack **e)** crowd **f)** bunch
3.

Proper nouns	Common nouns	Collective nouns	Abstract nouns
Mrs Green	chair	flock	misery
Julia	insect	gaggle	kindness
Thursday	train		
New Zealand	dog		
	boy		

Pages 10–11
1. **a)** Dad was very <u>proud</u> of his <u>fast</u>, <u>new</u>, <u>shiny</u> car.

b) The <u>rough</u> sea crashed against the <u>jagged</u>, <u>grey</u> rocks.
2. **a)** newer
   b) more / less beautiful / intelligent
   c) more / less intelligent / beautiful
   d) greener
3. **a)** Accept any sentence that includes **bravest** or **least brave**
   b) Accept any sentence that includes **worst**
   c) Accept any sentence that includes **most honest** or **least honest**
   d) Accept any sentence that includes **friendliest** or **least friendly**

Pages 12–13
1. **a)** possessive **b)** personal
   c) demonstrative **d)** relative
2. **a)** Preta ate a sandwich. **It** was delicious.
   b) Eliza danced for ages at the disco. **She** ached from head to toe when **it** had finished.
   c) Mum asked us to put our shoes on, but **they** were dirty.
   d) At my aunt's house there is a cat called Maple. **It** is **hers**.
3. **Any suitable pronoun is acceptable. For example: a)** who **b)** him / her **c)** it
   d) I; he

Pages 14–15
1. **a)** He couldn't see the tomato sauce <u>on</u> the table. (**place**)
   b) The baby ate <u>before</u> sleeping. (**time**)
   c) I looked <u>around</u> the room for a friendly smile. (**place**)
   d) I go swimming <u>after</u> gymnastics. (**time**)
   e) The troll stomped <u>across</u> the bridge. (**place**)
2. **Accept any suitable prepositions. For example:**
   a) in / during **b)** onto; off **c)** on
   d) after **e)** in **f)** on
3. **Accept any suitable prepositions. For example:**
   a) To score a goal, the ball must go **over** the line.
   b) The children ate their dinner **at** the table.
   c) We cycled **round / around** the lake.
   d) I put my shopping **in** the basket.

Answers

1. a) Shall b) could c) should
    d) would e) might
2. a) should b) will c) ought
3. a)–c) **Accept any suitable and grammatically correct endings.**
4. a)–d) **Accept any suitable and grammatically correct beginnings containing a modal verb and a noun.**

Pages 18–19
1. a) prepositional phrase
    b) verb phrase
    c) noun phrase
2. a) <u>The cat</u> jumped.
    b) Catch <u>the red bus</u>.
    c) <u>Poor Dorothy</u> coughed.
    d) <u>The car</u> broke down but <u>the old van</u> continued.
3. a) The classroom <u>has been tidied</u>.
    b) The experienced walkers <u>can climb</u> up a mountain.
    c) My dad <u>is cutting</u> the grass.
    d) This piece of jigsaw <u>does not fit</u> anywhere.
4. **Accept any grammatically correct and suitable prepositional phrases, for example:**
    a) The car broke down **during rush hour**.
    b) The children were playing **on the lawn**.
    c) The lights went out **at nine o'clock**.
    d) **Before bedtime**, I must put my bike in the garage.

Pages 20–21
1. a)–e) **Accept any suitable expanded noun phrases. For example:**
    a) Alex watched **the blaring** TV.
2. a)–e) **Accept any suitable expanded noun phrase to complete each sentence. For example:** a) Michael ran up the hill towards **his waving friends**.

Pages 22–23
1. a) The car stopped <u>abruptly</u> at the traffic lights.
    b) <u>Angrily</u>, Dad slammed the door.
    c) Zara waited <u>patiently</u> to see the doctor.
    d) The snow fell <u>heavily</u> as the children <u>excitedly</u> threw snowballs at each other.

2. a) loudly b) beautifully c) gently
    d) evenly e) smoothly f) lazily
3. a) urgently b) Nervously c) Slowly
    d) Carefully e) eagerly f) sneakily
    g) gracefully

Pages 24–25
1. a) The weather forecast says it will rain <u>every day this week</u>. (**how often**)
    b) The Smith family walk to school <u>extremely slowly</u>. (**how**)
    c) <u>Very loudly</u>, the orchestra started to play. (**how**)
    d) Lois and Kai played on the swings <u>at the park</u>. (**where**)
2. **Accept any suitable fronted adverbial phrases, for example:**
    a) **On velvet feet**, the cat prowled around the garden.
    b) **Out of the blue**, the gun went off.
    c) **Ten minutes ago**, he crossed the finishing line.
3. **Accept any grammatically correct sentences that use an adverbial phrase, for example:**
    a) I will read **tomorrow evening**.
    b) The dog barked **very loudly**.
    c) **Round the corner**, the parade was coming.

Pages 26–27
1. after a while, previously, soon, before, instantly, immediately
2. a)–c) **Accept any suitable adverbials of time. For example:** a) soon
    b) Previously c) next week
3.

Adverbials of time	Adverbials of possibility
soon	certainly
afterwards	possibly
seldom	maybe
next week	perhaps
last night	
all day	

4. a)–d) **Accept any suitable adverbials of possibility. For example:** a) possibly
    b) certainly c) Maybe d) probably

Answers

Pages 28–29

1. a) The baby drank some milk.
   b) The boy sat down until the bus arrived.
   c) Because he was tired, Jonah went to bed.
   d) I must wear my hat as it is a hot day.

2.

Main clauses	Subordinate clauses
• we will have a BBQ • our dog can perform tricks • I baked a cake	• before we left • if it is sunny • because we are on holiday

3. a)–d) **Accept any grammatically correct main clauses. For example: a)** After he worked all day, **he read a book**.

4. **Accept any grammatically correct subordinate clause. For example:** The girl cried **because she hurt her knee**.

Pages 30–31

1. Because the last bus had gone, I walked home; Although I like most fruit, I don't like bananas.

2. a) Yesterday, I went out with my friend, who is already twelve.
   b) The cakes, which were left on the table, were delicious.
   c) The Internet, which is a great invention, helps me with my homework.
   d) The acrobat, who performs impressive moves, will be on stage shortly.
   e) In the south of England, where the climate is usually warmer, the spring flowers are already in bloom.

3. a) which b) who c) where d) whose

4. **Accept any grammatically correct relative clause. For example:** The man, **who had just heard his daughter**, ran into the burning building.

Pages 32–33

1. a) The boy, who was cycling, was on his way to school, which was two miles away.
   b) The classroom, which is usually tidy, was a mess because the children had been painting.
   c) Because they were going to a party, the twins were allowed to stay up late, which was a very rare occurrence.

2. **Accept any grammatically correct complex sentences that include one subordinate clause, for example:**
   a) I didn't eat a mango **until I was ten**.
   b) **Because it was funny**, she laughed.
   c) The rhino, **which was huge**, charged at the men.

3. **Accept any grammatically correct complex sentence that includes two subordinate clauses, for example: Since it was raining**, I took the umbrella **that was by the door**.

Pages 34–35

1. a) The people, who were waiting at the bus stop, wanted the next bus to be red.
   b) An artist, who painted in the style of Van Gogh, once entered his work in an exhibition.
   c) A local choir beat a flautist, a clarinettist and a pianist to win first prize at the National Music Festival.

2. He wanted to buy a new car.

3. a) Although **the** tide was coming in, we still managed to have some time playing on **the / a** beach.
   b) On Saturday **the** weather will be humid with **a** thunderstorm likely.
   c) Mum asked us to shut **the** windows because **the** rain was coming in.
   d) **An / The** African elephant has larger ears than **an / the** Asian elephant.
   e) Our class went on **a / the** visit to **a / the** science museum in London.
   f) My sister screamed when she saw **a / the** large, hairy spider crawl across her bedroom.

Pages 36–37

1. I don't listen to anyone. ✓
   You're not going nowhere. ✗
   The baby can't hardly talk yet. ✗
   Don't get into any trouble. ✓
   You're not going anywhere. ✓
   The baby can hardly talk yet. ✓
   Don't get into no trouble. ✗
   I don't listen to no one. ✗

2. a) anywhere b) any c) anyone
   d) anybody e) anything f) anything

3. I am writing to complain about my recent visit to your hotel. When we first saw our room, we

Answers

were very disappointed. There was no space or **anywhere** to put our cases. The beds were small and did not have **any** sheets on. In the bathroom, the shower was not working very well and the bath was the dirtiest I have **ever** seen. Our towels looked dirty so we did not want to use them. When I tried to speak to a member of your staff, I could not find **anyone** to help me. I have **never** had **any** problems like this before and I hope you will give us a refund on our stay.

Yours faithfully,

Mrs Sams

Pages 38–39

1. a) and
    b) or
    c) so
    d) for
2. a) because
    b) Although
    c) When
    d) Since
    e) before
3. **Accept any grammatically correct clauses linked by one of the connectives. For example:**
    a) He rode his bike, **but I walked**.
    b) **Nobody was in when** I went home.
    c) The car stopped at the level crossing **until the train had gone**.
    d) **If you are good**, you can have an ice cream.
    e) At the show I won **and I cried**.
    f) There are not many people, **so it will be quiet**.

Pages 40–41

1. Tigers are beautiful. However, don't try to pat one.
2. a) Also b) however c) Consequently
    d) Firstly
3. a) to contrast b) to sequence
    c) to summarise d) to contrast
    e) to sequence f) to summarise
4. a) It's too late to go shopping. **Besides**, I'm tired.

b) Many towns are on a river. **For instance**, London is on the Thames.

c) We could go for a picnic tomorrow. **Ultimately**, the weather will decide.

Pages 42–43

1. a) active b) passive c) passive
    d) active e) passive
2. a) The chair was pushed over by Tamara.
    b) The mouse was caught by the cat.
    c) The guitar is played by the boy.
    d) Lots of juice is drunk by the little girl.
3. a) The burglar stole the television.
    b) The large beetle gobbled up the ant.
    c) The chef cooked the curry last night.
    d) The nurse bandaged my knee.

Pages 44–45

1.

Standard English	Non-standard English
Thank you very much.	It was dead nice.
I am happy with my work.	You're well cool.
The flowers are beautiful.	I did a good story.
Someone smiled at me.	I been bad.
	I've not got none.

2. a) I have not done anything wrong. / I have done nothing wrong.
    b) They were laughing at us.
    c) I am not happy.
    d) They should not have run away.
    e) I do not like those sweets.
3. She were naughty. ✗
    That ain't good. ✗
    I did not see anything. ✓
    They went to the seaside. ✓
    I isn't going anywhere. ✗
    This is the picture that I made. ✓

Pages 46–47

1.

Personal	Impersonal
a text message	a letter from the gas company
an email to a friend	
a note to your mum	a job application
a postcard	a police report
	a letter of complaint

2. a) **Accept any of the following**: The use of 'Hi' is too informal / personal; The use

4

of 'hasn't' is too informal / personal; 'Is that ok?' is too informal / personal; 'Love, Mr Burns' is too informal / personal; There are no complex sentences. / The sentences are all very short.

b) The letter should have correct grammar and punctuation, an impersonal greeting (e.g. Dear Sir / Madam) and sign-off (e.g. Yours faithfully), complex sentences, and formal, matter-of-fact vocabulary.

Pages 48–49

1. children is **plural**; cat is **singular**; men is **plural** (*1 mark for all three correct*)

2. The golden sand sparkled as the bright sun shone down. (*1 mark for both correct*)

3. I skipped in the school playground. (*1 mark*)

4. The doctor measured and checked her blood pressure. (*1 mark*)

5. because (*1 mark*)

6. **An** astronaut climbed into **the** space rocket. (*1 mark for both correct*)

7. More than one possible answer. Example: I love watching football. It is very good. (*1 mark*)

8. The people on the bus talk loudly. / The person on the bus talks loudly. (*1 mark for either*)

9. in (*1 mark*)

10. Michael's test results were disappointing. **He** felt sad that **they** were not better. (*1 mark for both correct*)

11. Despite being nearly twelve, I was not allowed to go into town on my own. (*1 mark*)

12. **Accept any grammatically correct complex sentence. For example:** Last night, while I watched TV, I ate some cakes. (*1 mark for subordinate clause; 1 mark for correct use of commas*)

13. an adverbial of possibility (*1 mark*)

Pages 50–51

1.

Full word(s)	Contraction
would not	**wouldn't**
is not	isn't

you are	**you're**
we have	we've
I am	**I'm**
let us	let's
we are	we're
I will	**I'll**
they would / they had	they'd

2. a) Tom**'s** jumper is too small for him.
   b) The giraffe**'s** neck is very long.
   c) The men**'s** toilets are out of order.
   d) This is Daniel**'s** coat.
   e) Mrs Javaid**'s** class is going on a school trip today.
   f) The girl**'s** pencil case was green.

3. a) Accept any grammatically correct sentence using **it's**.
   b) Accept any grammatically correct sentence using **you've**.
   c) Accept any grammatically correct sentence using **didn't**.

Pages 52–53

1. a) Please can you help me with my homework**?** It is quite difficult**.**
   b) How many weeks are there in a year**?**
   c) Did you prefer watching the film or reading the book**?** I preferred the book**.**
   d) When is it going to stop raining**?**
   e) Do you know when the library is open**?** I need to return some books**.**
   f) Although I am feeling brave now, how do you think I'll feel before the test tomorrow**?**
   g) Can you help me understand this report, please**?**
   h) How old was William Shakespeare when he died**?**

2. a) I don't really understand, do you?
   b) You did give your teacher the letter, didn't you?
   c) She has got the correct change, hasn't she?
   d) You were expecting me to arrive today, weren't you?

3. **a)–f) Accept any suitable, grammatically correct question tags. For example:**
   a) wasn't it?

Answers

4. **Accept any suitable, grammatically correct questions. For example:** Where did you buy stamps? Are you English? Have I got it right?

Pages 54–55

1. "Where's your homework?" the teacher asked. / "If you finish," he said, "you'll make me very proud."

2. **a)** Abbey said**,** **"**Don't worry**."**
b) **"**Nothing is wrong**,"** replied Dad**.**
c) "Maybe one day**,"** roared Josh**,** **"**we'll play football for England**!"**
d) "Help**!"** shouted the lost little girl**.** **"**Help**!"**

3. **a)** Holly said, "I can't wait to go on holiday next year." / "I can't wait to go on holiday next year," Holly said.
b) Alfie told his teacher, "I don't understand the work." / "I don't understand the work," Alfie told his teacher.
c) The reporter announced, "The restaurant has been shut down because of hygiene issues." / "The restaurant has been shut down because of hygiene issues," the reporter announced.

Pages 56–57

1. **a)** I like English, geography, science, music and art.
b) Newcastle, Liverpool, Hartlepool and Leeds are all in the north of England.
c) The Nile, Amazon, Mississippi, Congo and Amur are some of the world's longest rivers.

2. **a)** The children, who were all aged 10, played at the park.
b) The boy stopped talking, had a drink, then started again!
c) When we arrived at the airport, we found our flight had been cancelled.
d) I like skipping, but my brother likes football.
e) My friends are all going ice skating, but I have to go to the dentist.
f) Although I am good at spelling, I still need to use a dictionary sometimes.
g) Our school, which is one hundred years' old, had a special party.

3. **a)** two
b) three

4. **Accept any two grammatically correct sentences that are the same but with commas in a different place to change the meaning. For example:**
a) Before they left Anne, Sally and Megan waved goodbye.
b) Before they left, Anne, Sally and Megan waved goodbye.

Pages 58–59

1. The music concert (in the local theatre) starts at 5 o'clock. / The programme (about whales) was very interesting.

2. **a)** Washington **(in America)** is where the President lives.
b) Ice skating **(although it is a bit dangerous)** is lots of fun.
c) Galleons **(Tudor ships)** were very big and slow.
d) Erin is a great singer **(or so she thinks!)**
e) February **(often rainy)** is the coldest month of the year.

3. **a)–c) Accept any three of the following:**
Washington **– in America –** is where the President lives.
Ice skating **– although it is a bit dangerous –** is lots of fun.
Galleons **– Tudor ships –** were very big and slow.
Erin is a great singer **– or so she thinks**!
February **– often rainy –** is the coldest month of the year.

4. **a)** My birthday, on August 29th, makes me the youngest girl in my class.
b) The sun, normally hiding, was shining yesterday.

Pages 60–61

1. **a)** faltering train of thought
b) pauses
c) dramatic silence

2. **a)** Just then... the bell rang. / Just then the bell rang...
b) It was red... shiny... amazing!
c) "You could... you know... not bother," he said.

3. **a)** Jane Austen said, "We have all a better guide in ourselves... than any other person can be."

b) Charles Dickens said, "There is nothing so strong... as the simple truth."

c) Marcus Aurelius said, "Look back over the past... and you can foresee the future, too."

Pages 62–63

1. There are seven colours in the rainbow: red, orange, yellow, green, blue, indigo and violet. / Samantha burnt her hand on the kettle: she touched it when it had just boiled.

2. **a)** Dogs make good pets: they are loyal to their owners.

   b) Sophie liked watching sport; football was her favourite.

   c) We go to school five days a week: Monday, Tuesday, Wednesday, Thursday and Friday.

   d) The ice cream shop was fantastic; the other shops weren't bad.

3. **Accept any grammatically correct clauses that are related to the openers without explaining them. For example:**
   a) I went to France on holiday; you went to Greece.

Pages 64–65

1. **Any from the following:** to introduce a new section of a story; to introduce a new character; to introduce a new speaker; to introduce a new theme; to show a change in time or place; to introduce a new piece of information; to introduce a new point of view; to organise ideas and facts clearly.

2. **a)** A new paragraph starts on a new line.
   b) It makes the writing easier to follow / read.

3. **Paragraphs can be made as follows, though not all of them are necessary:**
   One day the wind and the sun argued over which one was the strongest.

   Spotting a man travelling on the road, they decided to play a game to see which one could remove the jacket from the man's back the quickest.

   Of course, the wind thought he would win with no problem at all. How could the sun blow off the man's jacket?

The wind began. He blew strong gusts of air, so strong that the man could barely walk against them. But the more the wind blew, the more the man pulled his jacket tight around him. The wind blew harder and stronger, but still the man pulled his jacket tighter and even fastened the buttons to keep himself warm. The wind blew until he was exhausted, but he could not remove the jacket from the man's back.

It was now the sun's turn. He gently shone high in the sky. The sun did very little, but quietly shone down upon the man's back until the man became so warm that he took off his jacket and looked around for some shade.

Pages 66–67

1. **T**he aeroplane will land in **M**anchester in forty minutes**.** (**1 mark** for both capital letters; **1 mark** for the full stop)

2. "Are you wearing your new shoes today**?**" Mum asked. (**1 mark**)

3. **F** in Friends (**1 mark**)
   The letter should not be a capital because the word **friends** is not a proper noun / is not the first word in the sentence. (**1 mark**)

4. "Stop it**!**" I shouted to my little brother. (**1 mark**)

5. Football**,** golf, tennis and cricket are my favourite sports. (**1 mark** for both commas)

6. A balanced diet**,** which includes fruit and vegetables**,** helps us to keep healthy. (**1 mark** for both commas)

7. The men**'s** coats were all too big. (**1 mark**)

8. **a)** shouldn't (**1 mark**)
   b) you're (**1 mark**)

9. The politician announced, "We will open new schools." (**1 mark**)

10. Sarah **(**aged 11**)** produced some excellent artwork in the style of Monet **(**a famous artist**)**. (**1 mark** for each set of brackets)

11. **Accept any grammatically correct complex sentence with a semi-colon used correctly. For example:** The weather was hot**;** the drinks were cold.
    (**1 mark** for correct use of semi-colon; **1 mark** for grammatically correct sentence)

Answers

Pages 68–71

1. That's amazing! **(exclamation)**
   I need a hat. **(statement)**
   Be quiet. **(command)**
   (*1 mark* for all correct)

2. The athlete <u>ran</u> and <u>jumped</u> really high.
   (*1 mark* for underlining both verbs)

3. **a)** How many sweets are left**?**
   b) There are six sweets left**.**
   c) They've gone**!**
   (*1 mark* for all correct)

4. **Accept any suitable adverb. For example:** roughly, loudly. (*1 mark*)

5. The fat, juicy burgers sizzled in the pan.
   (*1 mark*)

6. Claudia**'**s legs were aching after running up the hill. (*1 mark*)

7. I washed my hair. (*1 mark*)

8. Jane plays the violin *or* Jane is playing the violin. (*1 mark*)

9. because (*1 mark*)

10. **a)** The children were playing. / The child was playing. (*1 mark* for either)
    b) Mike was eating. (*1 mark*)
    c) The women were walking. / The woman was walking. (*1 mark* for either)

11. **a)** They've
    b) We're
    c) He's
    (*1 mark* for all correct)

12. Whoever (*1 mark*)

13. <u>The travellers</u>, who did not know each other, <u>all boarded the train together.</u>
    (*1 mark*)

14. The detective said, "There was a burglary this afternoon between the hours of 14.00 and 18.00, and I am looking for witnesses."
    (*1 mark* for correct speech marks and commas; *1 mark* for using the first-person singular in the direct speech)

15. in *or* through (*1 mark*)

16. semi-colon (*1 mark*)

17. **Accept any three suitable examples, for example:** a letter to an unknown person, a letter of complaint, a job application, an official report, a formal invitation, etc. (*3 marks*)

18. **Accept any adverbial of time. For example:** frequently, rarely, etc. (*1 mark*)

19. **a)** The cows are in the field. (**simple**)
    b) Even though it is raining, the cows are in the field. (**complex**)
    c) The cows are in the field and they are eating. (**compound**)
    (*1 mark* for all correct)

20. **Accept any two grammatically correct subordinate clauses. For example: Because it was cold**, I wore my hat and gloves, **which are very warm**.
    (*1 mark* for each clause)

21. The children played the instruments.
    (*1 mark*)

22. **Accept any grammatically correct sentence that uses brackets.** (*1 mark* for using brackets correctly; *1 mark* for the rest of the sentence being grammatically correct.)

Double negatives

2. Put a circle around the correct word to make each sentence correct.

a) He couldn't find his keys **anywhere / nowhere**.

b) Jessica couldn't find **none / any** of her missing jewellery.

c) I don't need **no one / anyone** to help me with my revision.

d) I did not meet **nobody / anybody** at the disco.

e) My teacher doesn't know **nothing / anything** about the argument in the playground.

f) I didn't do **anything / nothing** wrong.

3. Use the words below to fill in the gaps in the letter.

never	**anywhere**	**any**	**ever**	**any**	**anyone**

Dear Sir / Madam,

I am writing to complain about my recent visit to your hotel. When we first saw our room, we were very disappointed. There was no space or

_____ to put our cases. The beds were small and did not have

_____ sheets on.

In the bathroom, the shower was not working very well and the bath was the dirtiest I have _____ seen. Our towels looked dirty so we did not want to use them.

When I tried to speak to a member of your staff, I could not find

_____ to help me. I have _____ had

_____ problems like this before and I hope you will give us a refund on our stay.

Yours faithfully,

Mrs Sams

Conjunctions

Key to grammar

Conjunctions are a type of **connective**. They are used to connect words, phrases and clauses together. For example:

> I like apples **and** oranges.

> I like apples **but** not oranges.

Conjunctions come in two types. The **coordinating conjunctions** are **and**, **but**, **for**, **so**, **yet**, **or**, **nor**. They can be used to link **two main clauses** of equal importance.

> I like apples **and** I like oranges.

Subordinating conjunctions (**although**, **because**, **if**, **since**, **when** and many more) connect a **main clause** to a **subordinate clause**. Remember that a subordinate clause does not make sense on its own.

> I like apples **because** they are good for me.

Subordinating conjunctions can often come at the start of a sentence.

> **Although** I don't eat much fruit, I like apples.

Practice activities

1. Underline the **coordinating conjunction** in each sentence.

    a) He plays rugby and tennis.

    b) Joshua or Simon can help you.

    c) Take the umbrella, so we won't get wet.

    d) You should listen, for you might learn something.

2. Underline the **subordinating conjunction** in each sentence.

    a) Go along to the exhibition because it is really interesting.

    b) Although it is sunny, it might rain later.

    c) When it is my birthday, I will be eleven.

    d) Since you are still finishing your homework, I will play on my own.

    e) I want to learn how to ice skate before I go on holiday.

3. Using one of the conjunctions in the box, finish the sentences below with a **main** or **subordinate clause**. Use each connective once and remember that a clause must contain a **verb** and a **noun**.

and	but	if	so	until	when

    a) He rode his bike, _____.

    b) _____ I went home.

    c) The car stopped at the level crossing _____

         _____.

    d) _____ you can have an ice cream.

    e) At the show I won _____.

    f) There are not many people, _____.

Connectives

Key to grammar

A **connective** is a linking word or phrase. Connectives can link words, clauses and phrases together in a single sentence. They can also link together **different** sentences. In this way they add cohesion to a text.

> The train broke down. **Therefore** we were late.

The connective does not have to come at the beginning of the second sentence. It can act as a link to the first sentence from other positions.

> The train broke down. We were **therefore** late.

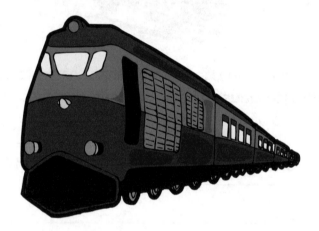

Connectives make writing more interesting and can be grouped into types according to their function. Here are some important types with examples:

Function of connective	Examples
to contrast	however; although
to add	also; furthermore
to sequence	firstly; finally
to give examples	for instance; such as
to show results	therefore; consequently
to summarise	overall; to conclude

Practice activities

1. Which example below is linked by a connective?

Tick **one**

Tigers are beautiful. However, don't try to pat one. ☐

Tigers are amazing. We should protect them. ☐

Tigers eat meat. Tigers can be dangerous. ☐

2. Underline the connective in each of these.

    a) The fair was exciting. Also, it was cheap.

    b) My brother played chess; however I watched a film.

    c) I went to the library. Consequently, I have lots to read.

    d) It wasn't a good idea to go. Firstly, it was too far away.

3. Look at these connectives and write whether they would be used **to contrast**, **to sequence** or **to summarise**.

    a) whereas   _____   **b)** secondly   _____

    c) all in all   _____   **d)** however   _____

    e) to begin with   _____   **f)** overall   _____

4. Use the connectives in the box to fill the gaps in the sentences below.

For instance	Besides	Ultimately

    a) It's too late to go shopping. _____, I'm tired.

    b) Many towns are on a river. _____, London is on the Thames.

    c) We could go for a picnic tomorrow. _____, the weather will decide.

Active and passive voice

Key to grammar

Sentences can use either the **active voice** or the **passive voice**.

The **active voice** is usually used, which means the subject of the sentence is doing the action. For example:

> ### The boy kicked the ball.

Here the focus is on the boy and he is the subject. The ball is the object.

Sometimes, however, the **passive voice** is used. In the passive voice the action is done to the subject. For example:

> ### The ball was kicked by the boy.

In this sentence the focus is on the ball. It is the subject.

Both sentences describe the same thing; the first from the boy's point of view and the second from the ball's.

Practice activities

1. In the space provided, write whether each sentence is active or passive.

   a) Chloe fed the cat. _____

   b) The cat was fed by Chloe. _____

   c) The school was closed by the head teacher. _____

   d) The journalists are writing reports. _____

   e) The meal was cooked by mum. _____

2. Rewrite these active sentences as **passive** sentences.

a) Tamara pushed the chair over.

_____

b) The cat caught the mouse.

_____

c) The boy plays the guitar.

_____

d) The little girl drinks lots of juice.

_____

3. Change these passive sentences into **active** sentences.

a) The television was stolen by the burglar.

_____

b) The ant was gobbled up by the large beetle.

_____

c) The curry was cooked by the chef last night.

_____

d) My knee was bandaged by the nurse.

_____

Standard English

Key to grammar

Standard English is generally formal English that contains correct grammar and punctuation with a range of sentence types.

Non-standard English often uses incorrect grammar and punctuation and is very informal. It is usually slang or colloquial language.

Practice activities

1. Look at the sentences and place them under either **Standard English** or **non-standard English** in the table below.

   It was dead nice. You're well cool. Thank you very much.

   I did a good story. I am happy with my work. I been bad.

   The flowers are beautiful. Someone smiled at me. I've not got none.

Standard English	Non-standard English

2. Rewrite each sentence below in **Standard English**.

    a) I not done nothing wrong.

    _____

    b) They was laughing at us.

    _____

    c) I isn't happy.

    _____

    d) They shouldn't of ran away.

    _____

    e) I don't like them sweets.

    _____

3. Tick the sentences that use Standard English and put a cross next to the ones that use non-standard English.

	Tick/Cross
She were naughty.	
That ain't good.	
I did not see anything.	
They went to the seaside.	
I isn't going anywhere.	
This is the picture that I made.	

Personal and impersonal writing

Key to grammar

When we write we need to be sure that the language we use is **appropriate**.

Either Standard or non-standard English can be used in **personal writing**, but this type of writing often has a chatty (colloquial) style and generally makes use of contractions, such as **I'm**, **isn't**, etc. Personal writing is used in texts such as blogs, emails, text messages and notes. Here is an example of the personal form:

> Watch out, guys! I've noticed over the past few weeks the restaurant's been overcharging people.

Impersonal writing, on the other hand, **always** uses Standard English. Contractions are not used and the language is often more formal, matter-of-fact and technical. Complex sentences are also common. Impersonal writing is used in texts such as reports, official letters and formal invitations. Here is an example of the impersonal form:

> Please be aware that it has been brought to our attention in recent weeks that the restaurant has been overcharging its customers.

Practice activities

1. Place the following texts under **personal** or **impersonal** in the table below.

    a letter from the gas company   **a text message**

    an email to a friend   **a job application**   **a note to your mum**

    a police report   **a postcard**   **a letter of complaint**

Personal	Impersonal

2. Read the letter below, which is addressed to the local council.

> Hi,
>
> Our bin hasn't been emptied. Can you tell me why not? It is overflowing and there is a lot of rubbish on the floor. It is making our garden look a mess. I need you to sort this problem out. Is that ok?
>
> Love,
>
> Mr Burns

a) Find **two** examples of inappropriate language in the text and explain why they are inappropriate.

_____

_____

b) Rewrite the letter to make it impersonal. You can add more detail, vocabulary and punctuation to improve it.

_____

_____

_____

_____

_____

_____

_____

_____

_____

_____

_____

_____

_____

Test your grammar

These questions will help you to practise the grammar skills you have learned in this book. They will also help you prepare for the grammar and punctuation test that you will take in Year 6 at the end of Key Stage 2.

Make sure you read each question carefully and do what it asks. The questions slowly get harder to help you progress steadily.

1. Write next to each word below whether it is singular or plural.

    children _____

    cat   _____

    men   _____   *1 mark*

2. Underline the adjectives in this sentence.

    The golden sand sparkled as the bright sun shone down.   *1 mark*

3. Write this sentence in the past tense.

    I skip in the school playground.

    _____

                                                                        1 mark

4. Which sentence contains two verbs?

                                                                Tick **one**

    The children played outside in the garden.   ☐

    The doctor measured and checked her blood pressure.   ☐

    The teacher marked some books.   ☐

    The Queen travelled by horse and carriage.   ☐   *1 mark*

5. Circle the connective in the sentence below.

    I laughed aloud because the story was funny.   *1 mark*

6. Circle the determiners in the sentence below.

    An astronaut climbed into the space rocket.   *1 mark*

7. Rewrite this sentence using Standard English.

    I love watching football, it's well good.

    _____

                                                                        1 mark

8. Rewrite this sentence so that the subject and verb agree.

The people on the bus talks loudly.

_____

1 mark

9. Circle the preposition that best completes **both** sentences below.

under   **in**   **up**   **down**

The girl ran _____ the garden.

The present is _____ the bag.

1 mark

10. Complete the sentence using suitable pronouns.

Michael's test results were disappointing. _____ felt sad that _____ were not better.

1 mark

11. Underline the subordinate clause in the sentence below.

Despite being nearly twelve, I was not allowed to go into town on my own.

1 mark

12. Turn the sentence below into a complex sentence.

I ate some cakes.

_____

2 marks

13. What type of adverbial is **perhaps**?

Tick **one**

an adverbial of place ☐

an adverbial of possibility ☐

an adverbial of manner ☐

an adverbial of time ☐

1 mark

Apostrophes

Key to punctuation

An **apostrophe** is used to show **contraction**: when letters are missed out to join two words.

> do not ⟶ don't   I have ⟶ I've   it is ⟶ it's

An **apostrophe** is also used to show **possession**: when something belongs to something else.

If the owner is **singular**, add an apostrophe followed by an **s** to the end of the word.

> Matt**'s** lunch   Amita**'s** book   the day**'s** events

If the owner is **plural**, and the word ends in **s**, just add an apostrophe after the **s**.

> the boys**'** lunch   the girls**'** books   the days**'** events

If the owner is **plural** but the word does **not** end in **s**, then treat it as if it were singular and add an apostrophe followed by an **s**.

> the children**'s** lunchboxes   the men**'s** books   the women**'s** events

Practice activities

1. Complete the tables below.

Full word(s)	Contraction
can not	can't
would not	
	isn't
you are	
	we've

Full word(s)	Contraction
I am	
	let's
	we're
I will	
	they'd

2. Rewrite these sentences using an apostrophe and the letter **s** where necessary.

a) Toms jumper is too small for him.

_____

b) The giraffes neck is very long.

_____

c) The mens toilets are out of order.

_____

d) This is Daniels coat.

_____

e) Mrs Javaid class is going on a school trip today.

_____

f) The girl pencil case was green.

_____

3. Using an apostrophe, contract the words below and use each word in a short sentence.

a) it is _____

b) you have _____

c) did not _____

Questions and question tags

Key to punctuation

Question marks are needed at the end of **questions** and **question tags**.

A **question tag** is a question added to a statement, exclamation or command that invites the person listening or reading to agree. Question tags are often used in informal English. For example:

It's a nice day today, **isn't it**?

Turn it down, **will you**?

Practice activities

1. Put question marks and full stops in the correct places in these sentences.

   a) Please can you help me with my homework It is quite difficult

   b) How many weeks are there in a year

   c) Did you prefer watching the film or reading the book I preferred the book

   d) When is it going to stop raining

   e) Do you know when the library is open I need to return some books

   f) Although I am feeling brave now, how do you think I'll feel before the test tomorrow

   g) Can you help me understand this report, please

   h) How old was William Shakespeare when he died

Questions and question tags

2. Underline the question tags in these sentences.

    a) I don't really understand, do you?

    b) You did give your teacher the letter, didn't you?

    c) She has got the correct change, hasn't she?

    d) You were expecting me to arrive today, weren't you?

3. Write a question tag to end the following sentences.

    a) The match this morning was cancelled, _____

    b) The doctor's surgery is very busy today, _____

    c) I love the sunshine today, _____

    d) I would love to go to the fun fair tomorrow, _____

    e) The new baby is very cute, _____

    f) Exercise is good for everyone, _____

4. Write a question to go along with the answers in the table below (the first one has been done for you). Remember to begin the question with a capital letter.

Question	Answer
How many cakes did you eat?	I ate four.
	At the post office.
	No, I'm French.
	Yes, you have!

Direct speech

Key to punctuation

Direct speech is what a speaker actually says and is written with **inverted commas** (also called **speech marks**) around it.

> "All dogs need exercising," Mum informed me.
>
> I replied grumpily, "I know!"
>
> "In that case," said Mum, "here's the lead!"

If a sentence begins with direct speech (like the **first** and **third** sentences above), we add a comma, exclamation mark or question mark just **before** the closing inverted commas, and then usually let the reader know who said it.

If the sentence begins by telling us who is speaking (like the **second** sentence above), a comma should appear **before** the speech begins. When the direct speech finishes, it should normally end with a full stop, question mark or exclamation mark just **before** the closing inverted commas.

Notice that a new paragraph starts when a new person begins speaking, and all direct speech starts with a **capital letter**, except where a sentence of direct speech is **broken** by information about who is talking (like the **third** sentence).

Practice activities

1. Which sentences are punctuated correctly?

    Tick **two**

    "Where's your homework?" the teacher asked. ☐

    "If you finish," he said, "you'll make me very proud." ☐

    "Oh, no!" The balloon has burst I cried. ☐

    Amy said "Let's have a drink" ☐

2. Add inverted commas and the correct punctuation to these sentences.

   a) Abbey said Don't worry

   b) Nothing is wrong replied Dad

   c) Maybe one day roared Josh we'll play football for England

   d) Help shouted the lost little girl Help

3. Write the sentences below using direct speech. Remember to punctuate them correctly.

   Example: Mohammed asked Zack if he would like to play tennis after school.

        <u>Mohammed asked Zack, "Would you like to play tennis after</u>
        <u>school?"</u>

   a) Holly said that she couldn't wait to go on holiday next year.

   _____

   _____

   b) Alfie told his teacher that he didn't understand the work.

   _____

   _____

   c) The reporter announced that the restaurant had been shut down because of hygiene issues.

   _____

   _____

Commas

Key to punctuation

A **comma** is used to separate items in a list. For example:

> There will be sandwiches, fruit, biscuits, crisps and cakes.

Commas are also used to separate words in a sentence. They can replace brackets and separate added information. For example:

> My school, which is close to my house, has a long driveway.

A comma can also go between two clauses to make them easier to read. For example:

> She arrived at the train station, but the train had already gone.

Some sentences change their meaning depending on where the commas are placed, so commas need to be used carefully in order to make the meaning clear and avoid ambiguity. For example:

> The people waiting who had tickets were let in.

> The people waiting, who had tickets, were let in.

Here only people with tickets were let in.

Here everybody waiting had a ticket and was let in.

Practice activities

1. Add commas to the lists in these sentences.

   a) I like English geography science music and art.

   b) Newcastle Liverpool Hartlepool and Leeds are all in the north of England.

   c) The Nile Amazon Mississippi Congo and Amur are some of the world's longest rivers.

2. Place commas in suitable places in these sentences.

   a) The children who were all aged 10 played at the park.

   b) The boy stopped talking had a drink then started again!

   c) When we arrived at the airport we found our flight had been cancelled.

   d) I like skipping but my brother likes football.

   e) My friends are all going ice skating but I have to go to the dentist.

   f) Although I am good at spelling I still need to use a dictionary sometimes.

   g) Our school which is one hundred years' old had a special party.

3. Beneath each sentence below, write how many people climbed the tree.

   a) After they left Dad, James and Alicia climbed a tree.

   _____

   b) After they left, Dad, James and Alicia climbed a tree.

   _____

4. Write two of your own sentences to show how changing the position of commas can change the meaning.

   a) _____

   b) _____

Brackets and dashes

Key to punctuation

Brackets, **dashes** and **commas** can be used to insert a **parenthesis** into a sentence. A parenthesis is usually a word, phrase or clause that gives additional information.

We often put a parenthesis in **brackets** (brackets are also called **parentheses**). For example:

> The dog was last seen **(by an eyewitness)** at the park.

If the brackets come at the end of the sentence, the full stop, exclamation mark or question mark normally goes **outside** the brackets. For example:

> The dog was last seen at the park **(by an eyewitness)**.

We might decide to use **dashes** instead of brackets if the extra information needs **more emphasis**. For example:

> The dog was last seen – **by an eyewitness** – at the park.

At the end of a sentence, only one dash is needed. For example:

> The dog was last seen at the park – **by an eyewitness**.

Commas can be used instead of brackets and dashes. They give less of a clue as to how important the extra information is. For example:

> The dog was last seen**, by an eyewitness,** at the park.

Practice activities

1. Which sentences below have **brackets** in the correct places?

Tick **two**

London the capital city of England (is very popular).   ☐

(The climate) is getting warmer according to conservationists.   ☐

The music concert (in the local theatre) starts at 5 o'clock.   ☐

Reading books especially non-fiction (helps you to learn).   ☐

The programme (about whales) was very interesting.   ☐

2. Add **brackets** to these sentences.

   a) Washington in America is where the President lives.

   b) Ice skating although it is a bit dangerous is lots of fun.

   c) Galleons Tudor ships were very big and slow.

   d) Erin is a great singer or so she thinks!

   e) February often rainy is the coldest month of the year.

3. Rewrite **three** of the sentences above using **dashes** instead of brackets.

   a) _____

   b) _____

   c) _____

4. Add **commas** to the sentences below.

   a) My birthday on August 29th makes me the youngest girl in my class.

   b) The sun normally hiding was shining yesterday.

Ellipses

Key to punctuation

An **ellipsis** is a row of three dots.

It is an important cohesive device and can be used to show a pause, a faltering train of thought, a dramatic silence, or when someone has trailed off mid-sentence.

Pauses:	Something moved**...** something small**...** something furry!
Faltering train of thought:	Well**...** we could do it**...** I suppose.
Dramatic silence:	Just then he stopped**...**
Trailing off mid-sentence:	I like it, but**...**

In formal writing, an ellipsis is often used to show where words have been left out of a quotation in order to make it shorter.

For instance, if a teacher says, "**All schools**, where parents trust that their children will be protected, **should be safe**," you could use an ellipsis and quote the teacher as saying, **"All schools... should be safe."**

Practice activities

1. Read the sentences below. Under each sentence, write whether the ellipsis/ellipses are used to show **pauses**, a **faltering train of thought** or a **dramatic silence**.

    a) "Nobody will notice if..." thought Sam.

    _____

    b) On your marks... get set... go!

    _____

    c) The door creaked... the floorboards squeaked.

    _____

2. Rewrite these sentences putting ellipsis/ellipses in a suitable place.

a) Just then the bell rang.

_____

b) It was red shiny amazing!

_____

c) "You could you know not bother," he said.

_____

3. Look at the statements below written by famous authors. For each author, write a sentence using an ellipsis that only quotes their **words in bold**.

Example: Some are born great, some achieve greatness, **and some have greatness thrust upon them**. (William Shakespeare)

William Shakespeare said, "Some are born great... and some have greatness thrust upon them."

a) **We have all a better guide in ourselves**, if we would attend to it, **than any other person can be**. (Jane Austen)

_____

_____

b) **There is nothing so strong** or safe in an emergency of life **as the simple truth**. (Charles Dickens)

_____

_____

c) **Look back over the past**, with its changing empires that rose and fell, **and you can foresee the future, too**. (Marcus Aurelius)

_____

_____

Colons and semi-colons

Practice activities

1. Which sentences use a **colon** correctly?

Tick **two**

There are seven colours in the rainbow: red, orange, yellow, green, blue, indigo and violet. ☐

Samantha burnt her hand on the kettle: she touched it when it had just boiled. ☐

Reuben liked the strawberries: Becky liked the cake. ☐

The sun was shining yesterday: today it is raining. ☐

2. Join the broken sentences with a **colon or semi-colon**. Write the completed sentences on the lines below.

Dogs make good pets	the other shops weren't bad.
Sophie liked watching sport	Monday, Tuesday, Wednesday, Thursday and Friday.
We go to school five days a week	football was her favourite.
The ice cream shop was fantastic	they are loyal to their owners.

a) _____

_____

b) _____

_____

c) _____

_____

d) _____

_____

3. Complete these sentences so that the **semi-colons** are used correctly. Remember, the second clause should not explain the first; it should just be related.

a) I went to France on holiday; _____

b) The teacher laughed; _____

c) Maisie read a book; _____

d) Water keeps us healthy; _____

Paragraphs

Key to punctuation

Paragraphs are used to help organise information in a text. They contain one or more sentences about an idea or topic.

In the writing of **fiction**, new paragraphs are used to:

- introduce new sections of a story
- introduce new characters
- introduce a new speaker of dialogue
- introduce a new theme
- show a change in time or place.

In the writing of **non-fiction**, paragraphs can sometimes start with a subheading and are used to:

- introduce new pieces of information
- introduce a new point of view
- organise ideas and facts clearly.

When writing, each paragraph should start on a new line. Paragraphs make the writing easier to read.

Practice activities

1. Write four examples of when a paragraph should be used.

   - _____
   - _____
   - _____
   - _____

2. a) Which statement below correctly describes a rule for paragraphs?

Tick **one**

Paragraphs should contain at least two sentences. ☐

Paragraphs should not contain more than ten sentences. ☐

A new paragraph starts on a new line. ☐

Paragraphs always have subheadings. ☐

b) Explain how the rule you chose above is helpful to readers.

_____

_____

3. Read the story below, putting a mark where a new paragraph could start.

One day the wind and the sun argued over which one was the strongest. Spotting a man travelling on the road, they decided to play a game to see which one could remove the jacket from the man's back the quickest. Of course, the wind thought he would win with no problem at all. How could the sun blow off the man's jacket? The wind began. He blew strong gusts of air, so strong that the man could barely walk against them. But the more the wind blew, the more the man pulled his jacket tight around him. The wind blew harder and stronger, but still the man pulled his jacket tighter and even fastened the buttons to keep himself warm. The wind blew until he was exhausted, but he could not remove the jacket from the man's back. It was now the sun's turn. He gently shone high in the sky. The sun did very little, but quietly shone down upon the man's back until the man became so warm that he took off his jacket and looked around for some shade.

Test your punctuation

These questions will help you to practise the punctuation skills you have learned in this book. They will also help you prepare for the grammar and punctuation test that you will take in Year 6 at the end of Key Stage 2.

Make sure you read each question carefully and do what it asks. The questions slowly get harder to help you progress steadily.

1. Rewrite the sentence below, adding a **full stop** and **capital letters**.

the aeroplane will land in manchester in forty minutes

_____

2 marks

2. Rewrite the sentence below with a **question mark** in the correct place.

"Are you wearing your new shoes today" Mum asked.

_____

1 mark

3. Put a circle around the capital letter that is **wrong** in this sentence.

My Friends are called Mia and Jessica.

Explain why the letter should **not** be a capital.

_____

_____

2 marks

4. Rewrite the sentence below with an **exclamation mark** in the correct place.

"Stop it" I shouted to my little brother.

_____

1 mark

5. Add **two commas** to make this sentence correct.

Football golf tennis and cricket are my favourite sports.

1 mark

6. Insert **two commas** in the sentence below to make it correct.

A balanced diet which includes fruit and vegetables helps us to keep healthy.

1 mark

7. Add an **apostrophe** to make this sentence correct.

The mens coats were all too big.

1 mark

8. Use an **apostrophe** and **contraction** to shorten these words.

a) **should not** _____

b) **you are** _____

2 marks

9. Which sentence uses **inverted commas** correctly?

Tick **one**

The politician announced, "We will open new schools". ☐

"The politician announced," We will open new schools. ☐

"The politician announced, We will open new schools." ☐

The politician announced, "We will open new schools." ☐

1 mark

10. Insert **two** sets of **brackets** so that the sentence below is punctuated correctly.

Sarah aged 11 produced some excellent artwork in the style of Monet a famous artist.

2 marks

11. Write a sentence that contains a **semi-colon**.

_____

_____

2 marks

Mixed test

These questions give you another chance to practise the grammar and punctuation skills you have learned in this book. They will also help you prepare for the grammar and punctuation test that you will take in Year 6 at the end of Key Stage 2.

Make sure you read each question carefully and do what it asks. The questions slowly get harder to help you progress steadily.

1. Match the sentences to their correct type.

That's amazing!	statement
I need a hat.	command
Be quiet.	exclamation

1 mark

2. Underline the **verbs** in the sentence below.

    The athlete ran and jumped really high.

1 mark

3. Choose a **punctuation mark** from the box below to complete the sentences. Each mark can only be used once.

.	!	?

    a) How many sweets are left _____

    b) There are six sweets left _____

    c) They've gone _____

1 mark

4. Complete the sentence below with an **adverb** that makes sense.

    The sea crashed _____ against the rocks.

1 mark

5. Which sentence contains **two adjectives?**

Tick **one**

The fat, juicy burgers sizzled in the pan. ☐

The pretty birds build their nests. ☐

The tall building stood next to the river. ☐

The fish and ducks swam in the water. ☐

1 mark

6. Rewrite the sentence below correctly using an **apostrophe**.

Claudias legs were aching after running up the hill.

_____

1 mark

7. Change this sentence, so it is in the **past tense**.

I will wash my hair.

_____

1 mark

8. Rewrite the sentence below in the **present tense**.

Jane played the violin.

_____

1 mark

9. Circle the **connective** in this sentence.

Our history work is interesting because we are looking at a range of artefacts.

1 mark

10. The sentences below are incorrect. Rewrite them correctly.

a) The children was playing. _____

b) Mike were eating. _____

c) The women was walking. _____

3 marks

11. Contract these words using an **apostrophe**.

    a) They have   _____

    b) We are   _____

    c) He is   _____

1 mark

12. Complete the sentence below with a **relative pronoun**.

_____ wins the race, will receive the medal.

1 mark

13. Underline the **main clause** in this sentence.

The travellers, who did not know each other, all boarded the train together.

1 mark

14. Put the detective's words into **direct speech** using **inverted commas**.

The detective said there was a burglary this afternoon between the hours of 14.00 and 18.00, and he is looking for witnesses.

_____

_____

2 marks

15. Add a **preposition** to this sentence so that it makes sense.

The audience waved their hands _____ the air to show their appreciation.

1 mark

16. What kind of **punctuation mark** is used in the **middle** of the sentence below?

Exercise is important for our wellbeing; we need to keep healthy.

_____

1 mark

17. Give **three** examples of when you would be required to write a formal piece of writing.

- _____

- _____

- _____

3 marks

18. Write an **adverbial of time**.

_____

1 mark

19. Read each sentence and write whether it is a **simple**, **compound** or **complex** sentence.

a)   The cows are in the field.   _____

b)   Even though it is raining, the cows are in the field.   _____

c)   The cows are in the field and they are eating.   _____

1 mark

20. Add **two subordinate clauses** to the main clause below.

_____ I wore my hat and gloves

_____

2 marks

21. The sentence below is written in the passive voice. Rewrite it in the **active voice**.

The instruments were played by the children.

_____

1 mark

22. Write a sentence that uses **brackets** for a parenthesis.

_____

_____

2 marks

Acknowledgements

The author and publisher are grateful to the copyright holders for permission to use quoted materials and images.

All images are ©Shutterstock.com, ©Jupiterimages, ©Clipart.com or ©Letts Educational, an imprint of HarperCollins*Publishers* Ltd

Every effort has been made to trace copyright holders and obtain their permission for the use of copyright material. The author and publisher will gladly receive information enabling them to rectify any error or omission in subsequent editions. All facts are correct at time of going to press.

Published by Letts Educational
An imprint of HarperCollins*Publishers* Ltd
1 London Bridge Street
London SE1 9GF

ISBN 9780008294212

First published 2013

This edition published 2018

10 9 8 7 6 5 4 3 2 1

British Library Cataloguing in Publication Data.

A CIP record of this book is available from the British Library.

Commissioning Editor: Tammy Poggo

Author: Laura Griffiths

Project Editors: Daniel Dyer and Charlotte Christensen

Cover Design: Paul Oates

Inside Concept Design: Ian Wrigley

Layout: Jouve India Private Limited

Production: Natalia Rebow

Printed by Bell and Bain Ltd, Glasgow

MIX
Paper from responsible sources
FSC www.fsc.org FSC C007454